Keanu Reeves

AN ILLUSTRATED STORY

DAVID BASSOM

HAMLYN

Author's Acknowledgements
The author would like to thank the
following individuals for their
assistance and support: Julian Brown;
Tessa, Michael and Danny O'Brien;
David Richardson; Kathleen
Cunningham; Sandra Elizabeth
Kibbey and the Keanu Fan Network UK;
James Cameron-Wilson; Anwar Brett;
Lawrence McIlhoney; Jerry Cheung;
Michael Cracknell; and of course,
Bridget Cunningham.

Picture Acknowledgements
Front cover picture credits; **Kobal
Collection/Richard Foreman/20th Century
Fox Film Company.**
Back cover top **Rex Features/SIPA Press.**
Back cover left to right; **Pictorial Press,
Aquarius, Rex Features.**
All Action 10 top, 44 bottom, 64, /Jean
Cummings 68, /Phil Ramey 16, /Paul Smith 5
right, 70 71.
Aquarius Picture Library 2/3, 9, 24/25, 27,
30, 33, 35 top, 39 centre, 40, 44 centre, 45, 48,
60, 69 top right, all on 76 and 77.
Ronald Grant Archive 4 centre right, 4 right, 5
left, 20/21, 22/23, 23 top, 26 right, 28 /29, 31,
32 centre, 34, 36/37, 38, 42, 44 top, 51, 72,
/Columbia Pictures 49 centre
Kobal Collection /Ciby 2000/Recored Pic Co/
photograph by Richard Blanshard 5 centre left
and 46/47.
People in Pictures 61, 69 top left, 69 bottom.
Pictorial Press 19, 32 bottom and top, 41 cen-
tre, 50 top, 52/53, 53 top, 53 centre, 74, 75,
/Zuffante/SF 80.
Range Pictures Ltd/Everett 18, 24 centre, 24
top, 26 left, 35 bottom, 39 bottom, 41 top, 43
top, 50 bottom, 53 bottom, 65 bottom, 66,
Takashi Seida 5 centre right, 62/63.
Retna /A Rapoport 4 left, / 6/7, 8 right, /Richard
Foreman 41 bottom, /George Lange/Onyx 10
bottom, 73 top, /Steve Granitz 4 centre left, 12
top, 14/15, /Dennis Kleiman 73 bottom, /George
Lange 11 top, /Tony Mottram 11 bottom, /Peter
Orth 17, /Susan Shacter 12 bottom, 13, 78/79.
Rex Features 39 top, 43 bottom, 49 top, 57
top, 57 bottom, 57 centre, 58 /59, 65 top, 67,
/SIPA 5 centre, 23 bottom, 54 /55, /1994
Images 56.
Tony Stone Images /Stewart Cohen 8 left.

Executive Editor Julian Brown
Assistant Editor Karen O'Grady
Production Controller Melanie Frantz
Picture Research Wendy Gay
Design Steve Byrne

CONTENTS

1234

First published in Great Britain in 1996
by Hamlyn
an imprint of Reed Consumer Books Limited
Michelin House, 81 Fulham Road, London SW3 6RB
and Auckland, Melbourne, Singapore and Toronto

Copyright © 1996 Reed International Books Limited

ISBN 0 600 58990 0

A catalogue record for this book is available from the British
Library

Produced by Mandarin Offset
Printed in Hong Kong

56789

▶▶

COOL BREEZE FROM BEIRUT

1

Cool Breeze
from Beirut

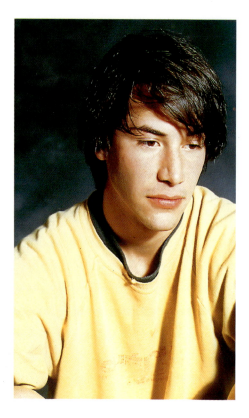

Above: Ḥawaii, the 50th state of America and homeland of Keanu Reeves' father, Samuel Nowlin. Keanu's name is Hawaiian for 'Cool Breeze over the Mountains'

Above right and opposite: Keanu initially wanted to be either an inventor or a racing car driver, but later decided to pursue a career as an actor

Keanu Reeves has become many things to many people

Noble innocent, romantic lead, no-nonsense action hero, gay icon, accident-prone eccentric, hunky heart-throb, promising bass player, spokesman for a generation and reluctant superstar, Keanu Reeves is many things to many people. During the course of his brief career, Reeves has charmed, captivated, amused, delighted and excited audiences across the world with a series of unpredictable and frequently surprising roles, while his offbeat and zany real-life exploits have fuelled many tabloid headlines. Both on and off screen and stage, it seems, the only thing you can expect of Keanu Reeves is the unexpected.

Although he lives under intense media attention, Reeves strives to maintain a low profile and keep his personal activities a secret. As a result, his life is characterised by contradiction, mystery and speculation. For example, the actor has lived out of a suitcase since he arrived in Los Angeles in 1986, yet refers to himself as a "homebody". He can command $7 million per movie, but prefers to work in low-budget, high-risk projects and play bass guitar in the unsigned band Dogstar for free beer. He has been hand-picked for roles by some of Hollywood's most acclaimed directors, including Francis Ford Coppola, Bernardo Bertolucci, Kenneth Branagh, Lawrence Kasdan and Ron Howard, but is constantly ridiculed by film critics. And, of course, he has been romantically linked with members

▶▶

Cool Breeze from Beirut

Right: A self-taught bass player, Keanu demonstrates his musical talent during a gig with his band Dog Star in Melbourne, Australia, November 1995

Below: Young Keanu's nicknames included "Ke", "Reeve", "Reevo" and "The Wall"

of both sexes by a series of increasingly outlandish newspaper reports. The list of idosyncracies is endless.

Reeves is almost always depicted as the real-life equivalent of Ted "Theodore" Logan, the good-hearted, dim-witted Valley dude the actor brought to life so brilliantly in the cult classics Bill and Ted's Excellent Adventure and Bill and Ted's Bogus Journey. Reeves's syntax is habitually disjointed and absolutely littered with words like "excellent" and "dude", and the actor might well show his approval by indulging in a bout of improvised air guitar. Friendly and unassuming, he is known to have a warm sense of humour, a healthy disregard for the trappings of stardom and a gift for self-depreciation.

However, beneath his exterior lies a drive and determination to refine and perfect his craft and avoid becoming typecast or pigeon-holed. Reeves's professionalism, enthusiasm, eagerness to please and dedication have impressed almost all of the actors and directors he has worked with. Either through master design or sheer luck, the actor has managed to constantly redefine his image with a series of eclectic roles and projects. Thus, the public have cheered him on as action heroes, swooned at his romantic antics, joined his search for enlightenment as the founder of Buddhism and shared his alienation when he portrayed troubled teenagers. While the actor does suffer the occasional setback, most notably in Bram Stoker's Dracula, the public are more than willing to forgive him.

Reeves's unique career reflects his equally exotic upbringing. The son of Samuel Nowlin Reeves, a Hawaiian-Chinese geologist, and Patricia Taylor, an English showgirl-turned-clothes designer, Keanu Charles Reeves was born on 2nd September 1964 in Beirut, Lebanon, weighing 8lb 5oz. Keanu (pronounced Key-ah-noo) was named after his great, great uncle and has two younger sisters, Kim and Karina. His first name is Hawaiian and means 'Cool Breeze Over the Mountains'.

Shortly after Keanu's birth, his family moved to Australia and lived there until 1966, when Samuel and Patricia decided to separate. Patricia took the children to the Upper West Side of New York, where she met her second husband, film and theatre director Paul Aaron. In 1970, the family spent a brief period in Australia before they moved to Toronto, Canada. Although Patricia and Paul parted after a year, the children became Canadian citizens and grew up in Toronto. Meanwhile, Samuel Reeves moved back to Hawaii and was occasionally visited by his son during school holidays. Keanu was 13 when he saw Samuel for the last time.

According to Reeves, his mother was "ahead of her time". She surrounded her family with culture and art and above all gave her children the ability to "love ideas." To make sure that they kept open minds, Patricia's offspring were raised with no particular religious or political beliefs. Although the family moved house five times in 15 years and Keanu changed school almost twelve times, the actor has always been quick to point out that he had a middle class, comfortable and secure childhood.

"When I see stuff in L. A. now, I realise how safe and sheltered my upbringing was," Reeves told Interview magazine. "We'd build go-carts called Fireball 500."

▶▶

At the age of six, Keanu had his first taste of things to come when he had his picture taken by a professional photographer, Richard Avedon. This marked the future pin-up's first 'photo-shoot'.

Keanu has frequently admitted that he was hardly an A-Grade student ("I even flunked gym," he quipped) and although he was popular with his classmates, he was considered disruptive by teachers. Fortunately, school did allow him to indulge his love of hockey and during his year at De La Salle College, he was named as the team's "Most Valuable Player". While his classmates nicknamed him "Ke", "Reeves" and "Reevo", on the ice-rink he was known as "The Wall", a reference to his admirable goal-keeping skills.

Halloween was one of Keanu's favourite holidays, because it meant that he would be provided with a "cool costume" courtesy of his mother. His outfits included Dracula and Cousin Itt from the Addams Family, while on one occasion, he played Batman with his sister, Karina, as Robin.

As a clothes designer, Patricia was not only responsible for keeping the family's Halloween tradition alive but also worked with numerous celebrities, many of whom, including Dolly Parton and David Bowie, stayed at her home. This of course, provided Keanu with his first experience of stardom and must have helped him formulate his ideas of how celebrities should and should not behave.

"There were times when groovy people would come over," Keanu told U.S. magazine. "Alice Cooper stayed at our house. I remember he brought fake vomit and dog pooh to terrorise the housekeeper. He'd hang out, a regular dude. A friend of mine and I, you know, wrestled with him once."

Surrounded by rock stars, Keanu became a regular concert goer during his early teens and his favourite performers include Husker Du, Joy Division, The Ramones, The Pixies, the Exploited, G.B.H., The Butthole Surfers, Fugazi, The Velvet

Underground, Wire, Sham 69, Discharge, Agent Orange, Big Black, The Clash and Emmylou Harris.

During the early part of his childhood, Keanu wanted to be either an inventor or a racing car driver, but by the age of 14, he had set his heart on a career as an actor. He made his debut in a highschool production of The Crucible, by which time he had already reached heartthrob status; when he delivered the line, "What am I?", his mother heard a girl in the audience reply, "A hunk"!

Keanu made a similar impact in Wolfboy, an offbeat play in which he portrayed a gay delinquent who seduces and then betrays the lead character. Events reach a somewhat disturbing climax when Reeves' bad guy is killed by his former-boyfriend, who then feasts upon his blood. The play caught the attention of Toronto's gay community and pictures of Keanu and his co-star, Carl Marotte, became collectors' items (presumably, they're even more collectable today!). Keanu's liberated mother, Patricia, apparently didn't object to her son's growing popularity with gay theatregoers, but hated the way that the photographer had managed to capture Keanu's acne!

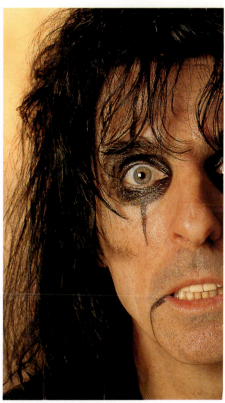

Top: Reeves was destined to become a male model from the age of six

Above: Alice Cooper, just one of the "groovy people" who stayed at Keanu's home

▶▶

Cool Breeze
from Beirut

Above: Reeves studied acting at Toronto's High School for the Performing Arts and Hedgerow Theatre before making his professional acting debut in an episode of the Canadian TV series Hanging In

In 1979, Keanu decided to leave high school to study acting. His mother offered very little opposition, and merely told him, "Do what you want to do." Reeves supported his fledging acting career with a series of jobs in Toronto, including ice-skate sharpener, tree trimmer, manager of a pasta shop and landscape gardener. While he missed out on a college education, he became an avid reader and his favourite authors include the likes of Dostoevski, Oriana Fallaci, Rimbaud, Diderot, William Gibson, Stephen Hawking ("one heavy dude"), Thomas Mann, T. S. Mann, Philip K. Dick, Jack Kerouac, Stanislavsky and, of course, Shakespeare.

A year after he left high school, Reeves appeared on television screens around the world as the thirsty star of a Coca-Cola Advert, and went on to promote Kelloggs' cornflakes. Looking back at this time in his life, the actor revealed, "I got a load of money, which I put into a basket and dipped into when needed." To his credit, Reeves has remained unashamed of his humble beginnings and has maintained that he only ever advertised products that he liked and approved of!

The year 1980 also marked Keanu's professional acting debut in an episode of Hanging In, a Canadian TV series set in a youth counselling centre. Although he only featured briefly in the show and had just one line, "Hey, lady, can I use the shower?", the actor considered himself "really lucky" to land the role and was pleased to add it to his resume. Perhaps more importantly, his wage packet helped him to buy his first car, a 1969 green Volvo 122, complete with seats held up by bricks!

In 1981, Keanu enrolled at Toronto's High School for the Performing Arts, where he intended to prepare for his stage career. However, although he was keen to act, he was never a great student and once again incurred the wrath of his teachers, who ultimately expelled him.

"It was a fun year but I got kicked out and failed," Reeves later explained. "I was rude and stuff – talking too much. Well that taught me a lesson when they kicked me out."

Having learned an important lesson from his experience, Keanu spent the summer of

1982 at Hedgerow Theatre in Pennsylvania, where he trained under Jaspar Deeter, a founding member of the famed Province-town Players.

Reeves also made his feature film debut that same year in The Prodigal, a domestic drama starring John Hammond, John Cullon, Hope Lange and Joey Travolta, which follows the effect Billy Graham's Evangalism has on the Stuart family. Keanu's appearance as a local teenager is so brief that the movie is often excluded from his filmography, but nevertheless helped keep the actor out of debt.

In 1983, Reeves played one of his favourite early roles, Mercutio, in a stage production of Romeo and Juliet. The play was directed by Lewis Baumander, who would help the actor bring Hamlet to Winnipeg some 12 years later.

Some 12 months after playing Mercutio, Keanu took one of his most embarrassing roles in the Canadian cop show Night Heat when he made a brief appearance as a hoodlum, 'Thug #1'. This no doubt helped

►►

him land the equally unpleasant role of "First Stereo Teen" in the TV series Letting Go. He appears for around 2 minutes, during which time his misbehaviour in a video shop annoys the show's main characters.

Keanu's fortunes improved slightly when he joined the cast of Flying, a low-budget and unmemorable romantic sports drama which was retitled Dream to Believe for international release the following year. Directed by Paul Lynch, the film follows the trials and tribulations of Robin (Olivia D'Abo), an aspiring female gymnast who is seriously injured in a car crash which claims the life of her father. Not only must she come to terms with the tragic loss, but must also overcome her physical and mental trauma to resume her career. Eventually, she wins a place in the school athletics team and fights for acceptance under the watchful eye of her tough-talking coach, Jean (played by British actress Rita Tushingham), before entering a national competition.

While Flying focuses on the relationship between Robin and Jean, Keanu co-stars as Robin's supportive boyfriend, Tommy, and clearly relishes the opportunity to prove that he can play characters other than hooligans and thugs. Although he doesn't join in with the gymnastics, he proves an irresistable romantic lead and wins the love of Robin with ease. Shortly after, Keanu made a brief and inoffensive appearance in an episode of The Comedy Factory.

However, despite his work on Flying and The Comedy Factory, Reeves was tired of playing thugs and hoodlums and increasingly felt frustrated by the lack of interesting roles that were available to him. By the end of the year, he became convinced that his future lay outside Canada.

"I wanted to go to Los Angeles and see if I could act there," he explained several years later. "I had the courage of youth."

In 1986, Reeves packed his belongings together and, with $3,000 in his money basket, left for the film capital of the world in his trusty Volvo to audition for a starring role in a Disney TV movie. Although he didn't get the part, the actor decided to stay.

Above: Although Keanu's good looks made him an obvious romantic lead, he soon discovered that producers preferred to cast him as a troubled teenager

ALIENATION, ANGST AND ATTENTION

Alienation, Angst and Attention

For an aspiring actor, Keanu Reeves' early months in Los Angeles were "a terrible, terrible phase"

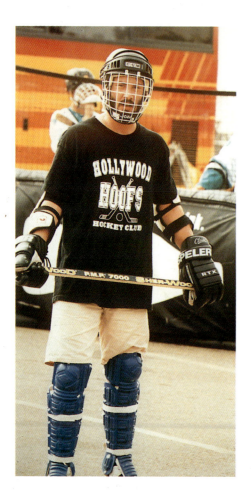

Keanu has maintained his love for hockey, demonstrating his skills on the ice rink in the Brat Pack movie *Youngblood*

During his first few months in Los Angeles, Keanu stayed with his former step-father, Paul Aaron, on Sunset Boulevard. While he searched for that all-important "big break", he worked behind the camera as a production assistant on one of Aaron's films.

Reeves refers to this time of his life as a "terrible, terrible phase". On his very first day in the city, the six-foot leading man-for-hire received calls from his manager and his agent, who both informed him that they were having difficulties getting him audition places because his first name, Keanu, "had an ethnicity that they found was getting in the way". Consequently, the actor came up with a number of pseudonyms, including Page Templeton III, Chuck Spidina and K. C. Reeves. Although he used K. C. Reeves for many casting calls, the actor always introduced himself to prospective employers as Keanu Reeves, and dropped all the pseudonyms within five weeks of his arrival.

At 21, Keanu looked and behaved about five years younger than he really was and landed a string of teen roles during the course of 1986, bringing him to the attention of Hollywood producers and directors.

In box office terms, *Youngblood* certainly provided him with the most exposure. Best described as "the Brat Pack on ice", the film stars former teen idol Rob Lowe as Dean Youngblood, a cocky hockey player (with Lowe in the role, how could he possible avoid being arrogant?) who leaves his family to join a small-time Canadian hockey team.

Youngblood then discovers that he must win the respect of his teammates and finds romance with the coach's daughter, Jessie Chadwick (Cynthia Gibb). Patrick Swayze (of *Dirty Dancing* and *Ghost* fame) co-stars as Derek Sutton, Youngblood's reliable best friend, while the virtually unknown George Finn steals every scene he's in with his portrayal of Youngblood's arch rival, Racki.

An unimaginative and predictable show-case for Lowe (whose career was beginning to wind down), *Youngblood* might not have won any awards but certainly didn't lose any money. While the film offered Keanu his first taste of big-budget, Hollywood film-making, he only had a few lines as Heaver, a member of the local ice hockey club. Nevertheless, the movie did allow "The Wall" to return to the ice rink and show off his hockey skills which, unsurprisingly, far exceeded that of the film's leading man.

Reeves found himself starring opposite another member of the Brat Pack, Kiefer Sutherland, in *The Brotherhood of Justice*, a feature-length pilot for a proposed TV series. Directed by Charles Braverman and written by Jeffrey Bloom and Noah Jubelirer, this routine drama presented Reeves with his first leading role as Derick, a privileged high school student who decides to take a stand against school violence and forms a group of underground vigilantes known as – yup, you guessed it – "The Brotherhood of Justice".

Although its members initially just observe school activities, things quickly get

Reeves starred alongside Lori Laughlin and Kiefer Sutherland in the ABC Sunday night movie, *The Brotherhood of Justice*. After the film aired, the actor was briefly touted as the latest member of the "Brat Pack"

out of hand and the Brotherhood eventually becomes another violent gang. Victor (Sutherland) implores Derick to stop the group and convinces him to take responsibility for his actions.

Although *The Brotherhood of Justice* won few admirers and didn't win sufficient ratings to be picked up as a series, Keanu delivered an extremely promising performance and managed to hold his own against Sutherland, his more experienced co-star.

After the film, Reeves found himself being touted as the latest member of the Brat Pack, something he fought to avoid.

Thus, whilst he has frequently confessed admiration and respect for the group of young stars who "really set a path" for all aspiring young actors, Reeves frequently stated that he had "nothing to do with them". Given the less than impressive careers of Judd Nelson, Andrew McCarthy, the aforementioned Mr Lowe, Molly Ringwald et al during the Nineties, this was the first of Keanu's many inspired career choices.

While *The Brotherhood of Justice* represented an important step for Keanu's career, the HBO TV movie *Act of Vengeance* represented something of a setback. Based on

▶▶

When asked about his role in the acclaimed TV movie *Under the Influence*, all Reeves could remember was the eight o'clock start

the true story of Jock Yablonski, the film boasted one of Charles Bronson's all-time best performances as the heroic strike leader, but was pretty cruel to Reeves, who found himself yet again playing another psychotic assassin, Buddy Palmer, in a mercifully brief role.

Reeves has little recollection of his role in the acclaimed TV movie *Under the Influence*. When a journalist for *US* magazine asked him about it in 1995, all the actor could remember was the eight o'clock start. "I thought this was . . . unfair," he explained. "It's hard to act in the morning. This muse isn't even awake."

Directed by Thomas Carter, *Under The Influence* is a moving domestic drama in which family man Noah Talbot (Andy Griffith) gradually comes to terms with the fact that he is an alcoholic. A powerful and insightful look at the condition, written by former-alcoholic Joyce Rebeta-Burditt, *Under The Influence* featured Reeves as Noah's son, Eddie, another troubled teenager.

Keanu's next project, *Young Again* provided the perfect antidote to all of his tormented roles. A gentle, warm-hearted and romantic spin on *Back to the Future* produced by Disney's television division, *Young Again* is a romantic comedy in which carefree 40-year-old bachelor Michael Riley (Robert Urich) finds that his wish to be 17 is granted when he is transformed into a teenager (enter Keanu!). He returns to the high school where he fell in love with Laura Gordon (Lyndsay Wagner) and realises that he still cares for her. After having a great deal of fun, Michael realises that he can't re-live his lost youth and decides to make a new start with Laura (Lindsey Wagner), who is

now a widow with two children. While screen veterans Urich and Wagner both deliver typically fine performances, Reeves (credited under his favourite pseudonym, K. C. Reeves) steals the show as 17-year-old Michael, and captures the born again teenager's energy, euphoria and delight brilliantly.

During the Christmas season, Reeves returned to American TV screens in *Babes in Toyland*, a whimsical, feel-good slice of family fun and fantasy. The third adaptation of the Victor Herbert operetta, *Babes in Toyland* teamed Reeves with wild-child Drew Barrymore who, he was pleased to say, was "off drugs" at the time.

Barrymore plays Lisa Piper, an 11-year-old girl who is too busy with her domestic chores to play with toys. Until, that is, she is transported to Toyland on Christmas Eve. When she discovers that the evil Barnaby Barnacle (Richard Mulligan) intends to seize control of Toyland, she joins forces with Jack Be Nimble (Reeves), Mary Contrary (Jill Schoelen) and Georgie Porgie (Googy Gress) and turns to the all-powerful Toymaster (Pat Morita) for assistance.

At 2½ hours, Clive Donner's version of *Babes in Toyland* lasted twice as long as the original adaptation starring Laurel and Hardy, and was only half as good. Still, the telemovie boasts a pleasing score and Reeves is obviously at ease not only as Jack Be Nimble but also the character's real-world alter-ego, Alex.

Reeves certainly kept himself busy in 1986, and could be seen on the big and small screens throughout the year. However, it wasn't until the release of *River's Edge* that people really began to notice his potential.

The year 1986 proved to be one of Keanu's busiest and his hard work paid off when he was cast as Matt in *River's Edge*

▶▶

LIVING ON THE EDGE

3

**Although *River's Edge*
received a mixed reaction from
cinemagoers, Reeves felt that
the film was "exceptional"**

Living on the Edge

When a dead girl's body is discovered at the edge of a river bank, high-school student Samson (David Roebuck) makes no secret of the fact that he is the murderer. While Layne (Crispin Glover) is determined to protect Samson, the rest of his friends are either indifferent or too spaced out to care. Eventually, after a great deal of soul searching, Matt (Reeves) secretly informs the police, thus forcing Layne to go into hiding with Feck (Dennis Hopper), an eccentric one-legged former biker.

River's Edge makes no effort to entertain or comfort its audience, which probably explains why most people decided to give it a miss. Nevertheless, the film received great reviews and has subsequently become a cult classic. Reeves himself has frequently sung the movie's praises. "I think the film is exceptional," he said. "It's great cinema."

The actor won the role of Matt following a standard audition and was drawn to the film by its "great script" and "great cast" and "the chance to be around Dennis Hopper". Although Hopper and Crispin Glover play the more striking roles of Layne and Feck, the film actually served Keanu best, who won acclaim for his raw and genuine performance and found himself under the media spotlight for the first time in his career.

River's Edge also brought him to the attention of director Ron Nyswaner, who was searching for a teen lead for his offbeat comedy/drama, The Prince of Pennsylvania. However, although Tim Hunter's film beautifully illustrated Keanu's understanding of teenage angst, it offered little hint of his penchant for comedy.

"I loved Keanu in River's Edge but it was a very serious drama and I had no idea whether or not he could be funny," explained Nyswaner. "So I had him up to the hotel in L.A. to talk about the part, and he made us laugh for a solid 45 minutes. After that, I knew he would be ideal."

Based on a true story, River's Edge was arguably one of the most important and influential teen movies produced during the Eighties. Directed by Tim Hunter, the film presents a depressing, downbeat, uncompromising, cold and occasionally offbeat look at alienated youth and offered a very stark contrast to Stand By Me, director Rob Reiner's sentimental and uplifting pre-teen road movie (starring River Phoenix) which also reached cinemas in 1986.

Top: Matt (Reeves) and Layne (Crispin Glover) confront Samson in River's Edge

Above: While River's Edge was an ensemble piece, it brought Keanu to the attention of several directors, including Ron Nyswaner and Kathryn Bigelow

Opposite: Reeves gives a raw and genuine performance as the permanently stoned Matt

Top and above: In The Prince of Pennsylvania Keanu demonstrated his penchant for comedy

Right: Keanu found himself cast as yet another angst-ridden teenager, Chris Townsend, in Permanent Record

The Prince of Pennsylvania is set in the coal-mining town of Mars, Pennsylvania, where Rupert Marshetta (Reeves) finds himself increasingly at odds with his militant right-wing father, Gary (Fred Ward), and his adulterous mother, Pam (Bonnie Bedelia), over his future. While Gary wants his son to follow him into the mines, Rupert has other career plans and decides to kidnap his father and hold him to ransom. Things go from bad to worse, however, when Rupert discovers that no-one is willing to pay for Gary's safe return.

It was inevitable that Nyswaner's quirky rites of passage tale garnered a mixed reception. While Variety described the film as "a gem of independent film-making", most viewers couldn't respond and spent most of the time wondering whether they should laugh or cry. Nevertheless, the film contains a plethora of witty one-liners and boasts two strong performances, from Reeves and Ward, who both make the most of the movie's comic and dramatic potential.

Keanu had an enjoyable experience making the film and particularly enjoyed

working not only with Ward but also along-side Amy Madigan, who played Rupert's girlfriend, Carla. It was also around this time that Reeves began his love affair with motor-cycling. He rented a Harley Davidson during shooting and spent most evenings driving through Pennsylvania with his lights off. "It was very cool," he later admitted.

Permanent Record featured Keanu as yet another troubled teenager and proved to be his first significant box-office flop in the States. In this contemporary drama, he plays Chris Townsend, a high school student who is forced to re-evaluate his life when his best friend, David Sinclair (Alan Boyce), commits suicide without warning or explanation.

Although Permanent Record attempts to explore the age-old themes of teenage angst and alienation, it lacks the courage of its convictions and ultimately comes across as a bland, superficial and sanitised varia-tion on River's Edge. Reeves's thoughtful and moving performance is the film's only strength, but cannot compensate for a dis-tinctly lacklustre script and poor supporting characters.

▶▶

Living on the Edge

Above: Although The Night Before was a comic showcase for Keanu, he alone could not compensate for the film's unexceptional script

Above right: In Dangerous Liaisons, Chevalier Danceny (Reeves) falls in love with his student, Cecile de Volanges (Uma Thurman)

Reeves's next outing, The Night Before, fared little better with cinemagoers and critics alike. Loosely inspired by the hugely successful Matthew Broderick vehicle Ferris Bueller's Day Off, the film toplines Reeves as Winston Connelly, a hung-over nerd who awakens in the middle of an alley with little memory of what happened during the eponymous 'night before'. Thanks to a series of flashbacks, Connelly gradually remembers that he was heading to the School Prom with his date, Tara Mitchell (Lori Loughlin), when a series of incredible events forced him to sell Tara to a vicious pimp, Tito (Trinidad Silva).

Inoffensive but unmemorable popcorn-fodder, The Night Before once again provided a showcase for Reeves, who frequently rises above an unexceptional script and provides some great comic moments. Off the screen, Keanu spent much of his spare time driving around Los Angeles on a newly purchsed Moto Guzzi motorbike, which he named the "Guzzi Moto".

Given Reeves' love of motorcycling and risky driving, it comes as little surprise that the actor has faced numerous police charges and had several accidents. He has one scar which extends from his navel to his chest and another on his calf, and nonchalantly admitted, "My body's a wreck." Ironically, the actor was in hospital recovering from one of his many accidents when he learned that he had won the role of Chevalier Danceny in Dangerous Liaisons, writer Christopher Hampton's prestigious adaptation of Les Liaisons Dangereuses, directed by Stephen Frears.

A pre-feminist battle of the sexes set in eighteenth century France, Dangerous Liaisons follows the cold-blooded power games of two scheming aristocrats, the Marquise de Merteuil (played by Glenn Close) and the Vicomte de Valmont (John Malkovich). When the Marquise de Merteuil challenges Valmont to seduce the innocent Cecile de Volanges (Uma Thurman), he declines and instead chooses to pursue the virtuous but married woman Madame de Tourvel (Michelle Pfeiffer). Reeves co-stars as Danceny, a music teacher who falls in love with Cecile, only to be betrayed by Merteuil and Valmont.

Dangerous Liaisons gave Reeves his first opportunity to display his theatrical training to cinemagoers. Opposite the likes of Malkovich and Close, he acquits himself moderately well and captures his character's innocence and naivity to perfection. Although Reeves had to learn how to sword-fight for the role, the biggest challenge for him was the scene in which Danceny cries at the Opera.

"What a nightmare that was," the actor recalled. "It was like six hours of trying to cry. Stephen Frears came up to me and said, 'Can't you think of your mother being dead or something?' You're a method actor. Isn't there something you can do?'"

In-between film roles, Reeves managed to squeeze several television appearances into his busy schedule. In an episode of Trying Times entitled "Moving Day", the actor once again demonstrated his flair for comedy as Joey, a removal man who wants to be a ballet dancer. He also featured in an instalment of Two Lost Souls and played a "Mama's boy" in the PBS special entitled Life Under Water

As 1988 drew to a close, Reeves was blissfully unaware of how the following year would affect his career.

TED AND TOD'S EXCELLENT ADVENTURES

4

Ted and Tod's Excellent Adventures

"It was very special. Great fun. Great characters. Great situations."

While *River's Edge* had won Keanu Reeves critical acclaim and cult status, the surprise success of the film *Bill and Ted's Excellent Adventure,* coupled with the impressive box office performance of Ron Howard's *Parenthood,* transformed the actor into a bona fide Hollywood star.

Best described as a cross between *Back to the Future* and a Laurel and Hardy movie, *Bill and Ted's Excellent Adventure* follows the exploits of Bill S. Preston Esquire (Alex Winter) and Ted "Theodore" Logan (Reeves), two good-hearted valley dudes who need to make a "most triumphant" pop video to propel their band, The Wyld Stallyns, to international stardom.

Unfortunately, before Bill and Ted can begin the journey to fame and fortune, they need to pass their history test; if they fail, the pair will flunk school "most heinously" and Ted will be banished to Oats Military Academy in Alaska, thus bringing the aspiring musicians' careers to an abrupt end. Given that Bill believes that Napoleon is a "short, dead dude" and Ted thinks that Joan of Arc is "Noah's wife", the pair's chance looks slim and Ted's dad has already booked his son's flight to Alaska.

While the pair take a crash course in history, a mysterious benefactor named Rufus (George Carlin) arrives from the 27th Century to assist the dim-witted duo, and reveals that it is absolutely imperative for Bill and

Ted to stay together, as the Wyld Stallyns' music is destined to "align the planets and bring them into universal harmony, allowing meaningful contact with all forms of life." Thus, with the help of a time-travelling phone booth, Bill and Ted travel to various locations in time and space where they enlist the help of such historical figures as Billy the Kid, Socrates (pronounced "So-crates"), Joan of Arc, Sigmund Freud ("The Frood Dude") and Abraham Lincoln ("The Dude on the Dollar Bill"), who travel to San Dimas, California in 1988 to make their unique contributions to the pair's "most excellent" history presentation!

Bill and Ted were created as improvisation characters by Chris Matheson and Ed Soloman in 1983 at University of California at Los Angeles (UCLA). Realising the characters' potential, Matheson and Soloman wrote the script for *Bill and Ted's Excellent Adventure* only to find that none of the major film studios were interested in the project. Numerous studio executives informed the writers that no-one like Bill and Ted actually existed and that the film would never find an audience. The script was eventually bought by Warner Bros., who then dropped the project at the end of 1986 and sold it to the veteran producer Dino de Laurentis's film production company, DEG.

Director Stephen Herek, who had just scored a surprise hit with the low-budget

Above: The meathead messiahs Ted "Theodore" Logan (Keanu Reeves) and Bill S. Preston Esquire (Alex Winter)

Opposite: Bill, Ted and Socrates (Tony Steedman) discover that travelling through time isn't as easy as most people imagine

Ted and Tod's Excellent Adventures

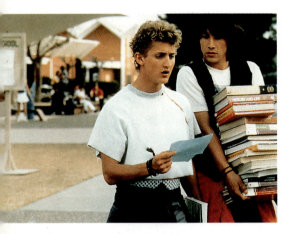

Above: When it becomes clear that Bill and Ted cannot pass their history test through study alone, the dynamic duo enlist the help of such historical figures as Socrates and Billy the Kid

Below: As a result of the film's success, Winter and Reeves became synonymous with the word "excellent"

horror film *Critters*, first became involved with *Bill and Ted's Excellent Adventure* in mid-1986 when the script was being developed by Warner Bros and it was his enthusiasm which pushed it into production at DEG. He was determined to minimalise the film's science fiction aspects and place greater emphasis on its comic elements.

"There have been a number of movies and television series that dealt with going ahead and back in time," he explained, "but this film is primarily about an unexpected fantasy come true."

Herek was also aware that the casting of Bill and Ted was crucial to the success of the film. Consequently, he auditioned hundreds of young actors during the course of a long auditioning process which lasted several weeks. On the final day of auditioning, Herek assembled 24 finalists and kept mixing and matching pairs until he found the ones he wanted and cast Reeves and Winter in the film's leading roles.

"Keanu Reeves and Alex Winter had never met each other until that day," said Herek, "but we could tell immediately they were exactly right."

To give the film a more offbeat and cult appeal, Herek assembled an extremely unusual supporting cast, including "Go-Gos" guitarist Jane Wiedlin, *Strange Behaviour* star Dan Shor, British actor Tony Steedman (whose numerous credits include *Coronation Street*), and popular stand-up comedian George Carlin.

Bill and Ted's Excellent Adventure began shooting in March 1987 and wrapped a mere ten weeks later. Most of the movie was filmed in various locations in Phoenix, Arizona, while some additional scenes were shot among the castles and coliseums of Italy. While the film was originally budgeted at an extremely tight $8 million, it actually cost $10 million to produce.

Bill and Ted's Excellent Adventure is a mindless and most triumphant comedy adventure, played to perfection by Reeves and Winter, whose brilliant on-screen chem-

istry more than compensates for the film's occasional inadequacies in the directorial and script department. Thanks to the pair of bumbling nitwits, the film is frequently hilarious and never loses its appeal. For instance, who could forget the inspired moment when Bill and Ted greet Rufus's arrival in a time-travelling phone booth with the immortal words "Not bad", or indulge in a spot of air guitar with their future selves?

▶▶

When Bill and Ted mount a "most triumphant" history display, an idyllic future is secured for the entire cosmos

Reeves had a fantastic time making the film and later said that the hardest part of working on the project was knowing if he was Bill or Ted. "It was very special," he explained. "Great fun. Great characters. Great situations. It was a remarkable time."

The actor studied cartoons to play Ted "Theodore" Logan and is simply faultless in the role. He was quick to point out that one of the film's strongest and most important elements was the friendship between the wo main characters Bill and Ted.

"Ted needs Bill because Ted is a child of the woods," he said. "Ted is a real dreamer, a bit naive, but always a positive and nurturing force within Bill and Ted's friendship. It may be Bill who figures their way out of trouble, but it's Ted who actually saves the day.

"Really, they are so connected, they're the same guy. They look at the world the

▶▶

Keanu Reeves joined the ensemble cast of director Ron Howard's ambitious comedy-drama *Parenthood* to play Tod, "the guy under the bed"

same way, and if one guy can't answer the question right away, the other will supply the answer. It's kinda scary – they're two dudes in a pod."

Promoted as "Equal parts Mark Twain, Monty Python and rock 'n' roll", *Bill and Ted's Excellent Adventure* was in pre-production and due for an Autumn 1987 release when DEG was declared bankrupt. Stephen Herek searched for an alternative distributor for the film and was eventually offered a co-deal with Orion and Nelson Entertainment; Orion would open the film theatrically and then Nelson would be in charge of the video

release. Thus, nearly two years after it was filmed, *Bill and Ted's Excellent Adventure* had its world premiere on February 22nd 1989 and became a surprise hit around the world, grossing $45 million in the United States alone.

Naturally, the film's leading men found themselves under intense media attention. Reeves became one of the world's leading teen pin-ups virtually overnight and found himself being portrayed not as an ambitious and promising young actor but as an amiable and harmless Valley dude; in other words, Ted "Theodore" Logan in real life.

▶▶

Ted and Tod's Excellent Adventures

"Party on dudes . . . Be excellent to each other"

"It was not my acting that gave me the reputation but my press," he later explained. "I'm a pretty wacky, goofy guy and I think I've been chastised by my personality, pigeon-holed because of who I am or who they perceive me to be, or the way I was. I make excellent good short copy because I use words like 'excellent'."

Reeves's co-star was also characterised as his on-screen alter ego, Bill S. Preston Esquire. "Every time I read interviews of mine, it is full of excellents, awesomes, totallys and radicals. I never use the words, they just end up getting injected into my vernacular."

While Reeves was frustrated by the "air-head image" projected by the media, he was embarrassed by his heart-throb status. Although he admits to being determined to stay in shape and keep reasonably fit, he is modest about his own romantic appeal. "I don't think I'm the most handsome guy in the world," he told *Sky* magazine, "but I know I'm not quite a dog."

Right from his "hunky" acting debut in *The Crucible*, it seemed obvious that Reeves was destined to become a teen idol, but it was much more surprising when he was labelled as a spokesman for a generation that had grown tired of materialism and dreamed of a society based on Bill and Ted's immortal instructions, "Be excellent to each other" and "Party on dudes". Although the film's underlying message that good things happen to good people struck a chord several years later in the highly successful Tom Hanks film *Forrest Gump*, Reeves was quick to dismiss Bill and Ted's relevance to contemporary society.

"I certainly didn't have a sense of myself – and still don't – as some cosmic spokes-man," he said. "Maybe Ted's an archetype, but to me he's merely a sweet slob."

A mere six months after the release of *Bill and Ted's Excellent Adventure*, Reeves was back on the big screen in *Parenthood*, an ambitious exploration of domestic life through the eyes of three generations of the Buckman family.

While the central focus of the film is Gil Buckman's (Steve Martin) determination to be a better parent than his own father (Jason Robards), Reeves co-stars as Tod, a good-hearted but dim Valley dude who falls in love with Julie (Martha Plimpton), much to the chagrin of her mother, Helen (Dianne Wiest). Directed by Ron Howard (*Backdraft*, *Apollo 13*), *Parenthood* is an underrated look at child-rearing featuring an extremely impressive ensemble cast, which includes not only Martin, Robards and Wiest, but also Tom Hulce, Rick Moranis and Mary Steenburgen.

Keanu plays a small but crucial support-ing role in proceedings as Tod. "I wouldn't say *Parenthood* is my film," the actor told MTV. "I'm the guy under the bed." Nevertheless, Reeves gives another charm-ing performance which won him several good notices. For example, *Variety* referred to Reeves's casting as "an inspired touch".

"It really was enjoyable," Reeves told *Sky* magazine about his experience making the film. "Ron Howard is a damned good actor and director . . . He gave me some really offbeat direction that was really 'actory'."

Once he had finished his work on *Parenthood*, Reeves decided to return to the stage and played Trinculo in *The Tempest* with the Shakespeare Company's winter workshop at The Mount in Lenox, Mass. Not only did this give him an opportunity to develop his acting skills but also allowed him to take get away from all the Hollywood hype and consider his future.

Intellectually-challenged but good-hearted Valley dude Tod finds that his romance with Julie (Martha Plimpton) is opposed by her family. Can't imagine why!

▶▶

THE TURNING POINT

5

William Hurt and Keanu Reeves
play a pair of incompetent
hitmen in *I Love You To Death*

One way or another, Keanu was determined to avoid being typecast

The dual success of *Bill and Ted's Excellent Adventure* and *Parenthood* was a double-edged sword for Reeves: on the one hand, it propelled him towards fame and fortune, but on the other, it threatened to restrict him to playing good-willed, charming but intellectually-challenged types for the rest of his career. For an actor who has always stated that he has no desire to repeat himself, the prospect of typecasting was horrific. To make

matters worse, to be typecast as a teenager would place a limit on the length of his career.

"If all you do is symbolise the youth of your time," he explained, "then you're going to burn out as soon as they grow up and there's a new youth in search of a new symbol. I won't mention any names, but that has happened to a lot of people."

Consequently, in 1990, Reeves began to move away from playing teenagers and

The Turning Point

started to pursue more adult roles. In Lawrence Kasdan's *I Love You to Death*, the actor decied to play Marlon, a permanently stoned hitman who, together with his alcoholic partner Harlon (William Hurt), is hired to kill Joey Boca (Kevin Kline), the cheating husband of Rosalie Boca (played by British comedienne Tracey Ullman).

"My guy was just harmless," Reeves explained later. "Larry Kasdan wanted this guy to be beat up by the world, just kind of in a daze. Harmless and drugged. So they hired me."

Based on a true story, *I Love You To Death* is a black comedy which depicts Marlon and Harlon's increasingly inept attempts to murder the seemingly indestructible Joey Boca. Sadly, the film's strong ensemble cast are let down by a script which is only sporadically funny. Overall, *I Love You To Death* is one of Lawrence Kasdan's most disappointing films and isn't in the same league as *The Big Chill*, *Grand Canyon* or even *Silverado*.

As in *Parenthood*, Reeves plays a supporting role and is only onscreen for about half an hour but nevertheless is terrific. The film led to his appearance in "The Tracey Ullman Show" and also marked his first collaboration with the late River Phoenix. Reeves told reporters that he had a great time making the picture.

"There were a few times when I was in the same room with Kevin Kline, Tracey Ullman, River and Bill and I would just laugh, just laugh out loud because I was so happy to be there with these great actors," he explained. "They'd go 'Action' and all this stuff would just go on and you'd be so alive. Amazing just to be there."

Incredibly, *I Love You To Death* features Keanu's favourite "hairstyle" (to use the term loosely), which he developed together with Kasdan and the film's hair stylist. "It ended up being like eight haircuts combined into one – a schoolboy at the back, shaved clean at the sides, a mohawk on top and this bit of hair just dangling down," the actor laughed.

Keanu's distinctive look, coupled with motorcycling antics, certainly made an impact on director Jon Amiel when he visited the actor to offer him the lead role in the comedy drama, *Tune in Tomorrow* (which was later retitled *Aunt Julia and the Scriptwriter* for international release).

"When I first met Keanu, his hair was shaved bald on one side and long on the other other," recalled Amiel. "The hair had time to grow before rehearsals, but on the first day he turned up swathed in bandages and was limping after yet another tumble off his motorbike."

Set in 1951, *Tune in Tomorrow* stars Keanu as Martin Loader, a 21-year-old radio newswriter who falls in love with 36-year-old Julia (Barbara Hershey), his uncle's wife's sister. Although Julia is looking for a third rich husband, she gradually succumbs to Martin's earnest and forthright charm and defies her family's wishes to date him. Their troubled romance is followed by Pedro Carmichael (Peter Falk), an eccentric scriptwriter who develops their story into a top-rated daily radio drama.

Tune in Tomorrow was shot on location in Wilmington, North Carolina, Paris and New Orleans. In the last location, the cast had a close encounter with Hurricane Hugo. "Hurricane Hugo missed us only by a mile," explained Reeves, "it blew off the second story of a building near us."

While it lacks the satirical edge of Mario Vargas Lloyd's novel, *Tune in Tomorrow* is a mildly entertaining romantic farce greatly enhanced by the top-notch performances of its two lead actors. For his first serious adult (or at least semi-adult) role, Reeves manages to transform himself into an extremely believable middle-class male, complete with starched shirt, collar, tie and short, conservative haircut.

Reeves won almost universal acclaim for his performance (*Variety* described him as "outstanding") and also developed a generally convincing New Orleans accent which he maintained off set. Ironically, the film

Top: As unbelievable as it sounds, *I Love You To Death* features Keanu's favourite hairstyle

Centre: Martin Loader (Reeves) tries to woo his aunt Julia (Barbara Hershey) in *Tune in Tomorrow*

Bottom: Martin turns to Pedro Carmichael (Peter Falk) for advice

Above: Adrenaline junkies
Johnny Utah (Reeves) and Bodhi
(Patrick Swayze) push each other
to the limit in the high-octane
actioner *Point Break*

also allowed Reeves to ride and crash a
motorbike, a scene that looks completely
believable and could hardly have been a
problem for the accident-prone real-life
motorcyclist.

However, in spite of Keanu's best efforts,
Tune in Tomorrow became the first film the
actor had worked on which required re-
cutting and several re-shoots after test
audiences gave it a big "thumbs down".
Even in its modified form, the film was a flop
at the American box office and went straight
to video elsewhere.

Having proved that he could play roman-

tic leads with as much ease as he could limn
"Valley dudes" and troubled teenagers,
Reeves was required to re-define himself
once again to star as an "adrenaline junkie"
in *Point Break*. Directed by Kathryn Bigelow
(*Blue Steel*, *Strange Days*), *Point Break* is a
high-octane, testosterone-charged, action-
packed thriller in which Reeves plays
Johnny Utah, a former football hero-turned-
FBI agent who poses as a surfer to track
down a group of professional bank robbers,
the 'Ex-Presidents' (so called because they
wear masks of Ronald Reagan, Richard
Nixon, John Carter and Gerald Ford during

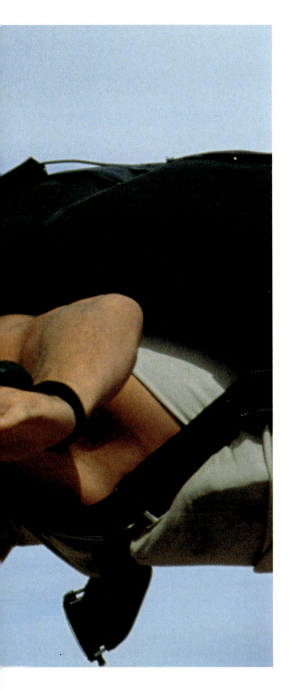

their heists). Whilst undercover, Utah is befriended by Tyler (Lori Petty) who in turn introduces him to Bodhi, the charismatic leader of a group of thrill-seeking surfers. Although Utah suspects that a group of Nazis are the bank robbers, he later discovers that Bodhi's group are in fact the culprits.

Originally titled *Riders on the Storm*, *Point Break* was written with Matthew Broderick (of *Ferris Bueller's Day Off* fame) in mind for the role of Johnny Utah, until Bigelow saw Keanu Reeves in *Rivers Edge*. As far as she was concerned, the film marked a turning point for the 25-year-old

actor. "The role was a departure from the work he's done in the past," she said. "He's never played an action hero."

Ironically, while most people would share Bigelow's view of Johnny Utah as an "action hero" and would class him as a prototype for Jack Traven in *Speed*, Reeves himself always felt that Utah was more of an "anti-hero" and that *Point Break* wasn't an action film but a drama, the focus of which is Utah's seduction by Bodhi and his gang of thrill-seeking surfers.

In order to play his first action/anti-hero, Reeves spent a significant amount of time with athletes, FBI agents, police officers and college students in fraternities. He learned how to surf (which subsequently became one of his favourite hobbies) and took a "crash course" in sky-diving so that he could personally film Utah's jump from 12,500 feet in the air. During the course of the film, Johnny Utah is shot, almost drowns, has close shaves with a vicious dog and an even more vicious lawnmower, is beaten up by a group of Nazis, and commits the *faux paus* of jumping out of a plane without a parachute. Thanks to Reeves, the hopelessly enthusiastic FBI agent manages to keep up with the action on land, air and sea.

Visually, *Point Break* is simply stunning: beautifully shot, crisply edited and boasting a number of stunning set-pieces, including the seemingly endless chase between Utah and "President Reagan" through numerous streets, back gardens and houses. Although the storyline is riddled with plot-holes (for starters, just why does Utah go home once his cover has been blown?) and the film definitely loses direction during its middle segment, Bigelow keeps events moving too fast and furious for most viewers to care.

In a situation remarkably reminiscent of *River's Edge*, Keanu's co-star Patrick Swayze (almost unrecognisable with bleached hair and stubble) plays the more striking role as the charismatic surfer Bodhi but the younger actor is the real winner in the long term, as *Point Break* demonstrates his potential as an all-action hero.

Point Break was shot over the course of an extremely challenging 77day period and the very day shooting wrapped, Reeves flew to Oregon where he started to rehearse for

The Turning Point

Top: Johnny Utah befriends Tyler (Lori Petty) as part of his undercover mission to find a group of bank robbers known as the "Ex-Presidents"

Above: Utah discusses the evidence with his FBI partner, played by Gary Busey

RIVER PHOENIX   KEANU REEVES

whatever it takes to have a nice day.

my own private IDAHO

A FILM BY GUS VAN SANT ⑱

Reeves risked losing his clean-cut, wholesome image by choosing to play the bi-sexual rent boy, Scott, in director Gus Van Sant's *My Own Private Idaho*

My Own Private Idaho. It's hardly surprising, therefore, that the actor joined the project feeling completely exhausted.

"I was beat. I didn't think I could get through it. But the spirit of Gus Van Sant, a brilliant director, and River Phoenix, a brilliant actor, drew me back into the fire."

Reeves and his co-star, River Phoenix, had met a few years earlier, when Reeves was working on *Parenthood* with Phoenix's ex-girlfriend, Martha Plimpton, and his brother, Leaf. They collaborated together briefly on *I Love You To Death* and agreed to shoot *My Own Private Idaho* together.

A low-budget contemporary gay adap-

tation of *Henry IV, Part 1*, *My Own Private Idaho* follows the lives of two extremely different rent boys, Mike (Phoenix) and Scott (Reeves). Mike is a narcoleptic prone to fall asleep at the most inconvenient moments and haunted by visions of his long-lost mother, while Scott is the privileged son of the Mayor of Portland who chooses to live on the streets as an act of rebellion against his rich family. When the pair travel to Italy in search of Mike's mother, Scott falls in love with Carmella (Chiara Caselli) and decides to return home with her to claim his fortune.

Named after a B-52s song, *My Own Private Idaho* is an experimental and far from successful road movie. Gus Van Sant occasionally delivers an interesting visual but is let down by his own screenplay, which goes nowhere very slowly. Unsurprisingly, the film was rubbished by reviewers and audiences stayed away. Even its admirers criticised it as being irresponsible for failing to mention, let alone address, the threat of AIDS.

While Phoenix won strong notices for his portrayal of Mike, Reeves received mixed reviews. The actor himself conceded that he was disappointed by his contribution to the film and felt that he could have done better if he hadn't been recovering from *Point Break*. Nevertheless, Reeves is once again absolutely convincing in the scene in which he has problems with his broken-down motorbike.

If playing the romantic lead in *Tune in Tomorrow* and the action hero in *Point Break* had the most influence on Keanu's career, then *My Own Private Idaho* was certainly the biggest risk he ever took. Reeves was warned that playing a bi-sexual rent boy could damage his clean-cut, wholesome image and end his rise to stardom, but was quick to dismiss such theories. "Hurt my image?" he would ask himself rhetorically. "Who am I? A politician? No, I'm an actor."

The actor's participation in the film did, however, launch widespread speculation about his own love life. Asked if he was gay by a reporter, the actor gave an ambiguous

The Turning Point

reply, "No... But ya never know." He subsequently explained his position when he stated, "There's nothing wrong with being gay, so to deny it is to make a judgement. Why make a deal of it? If someone doesn't want to hire me because they think I'm gay, well, then I have to deal with it."

Keanu's admirable refusal to shed any light on his private life has meant that he has been romantically linked with women and men alike. According to the tabloid press, his ex-girlfriends include Lori Petty, Paula Abdul, Sofia Coppola and an enigmatic lady known as 'Autumn'. However, the actor himself has stated that his career takes up most of his time and energy and as a result, he hasn't got enough time to have a "serious" girlfriend. "The only woman I see regularly is my sister Kim," he said. "If I need an escort, she's already ready."

Once Reeves finished shooting *My Own Private Idaho*, he travelled to Santa Clarita Studios in Los Angeles to reprise the role of Ted "Theodore" Logan in *Bill and Ted's*

Bogus Journey, the sequel to their excellent adventure. The actor had agreed to the sequel several years earlier, and the only delay was finding that ever elusive "right script". In the first draft, Bill and Ted kidnapped characters from famous novels to pass their literature test, and in the second attempt, they visited Heaven and Hell to rescue historical figures who helped them defeat their evil doubles. Both of these premises were considered too derivative of the original film and the scripts were banished to the reject pile. Fortunately, Chris Matheson and Ed Solomon's third attempt, originally entitled "Bill and Ted Go To Hell", was given the green light and the film started shooting on January 7th, 1991.

In the 27th Century, the evil De Nomolos (Joss Ackland) sends a pair of killer cyborgs to the past with orders to kill Bill and Ted before the Wyld Stallyns can win the San Dimas Talent Contest, thus changing their lives and the universe forever. When the heroes-to-be are murdered by the robotic

In *My Own Private Idaho*, Scott falls in love with an Italian girl, Carmella (Chiara Caselli), and decides to return to his family and claim his inheritance

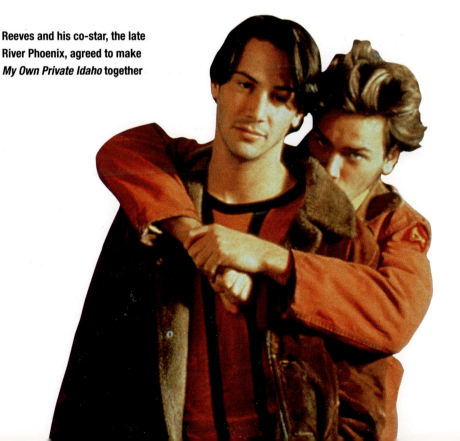

Reeves and his co-star, the late River Phoenix, agreed to make *My Own Private Idaho* together

The Turning Point

Top and centre: Bill and Ted meet the "Evil Us's" in *Bill and Ted's Bogus Journey*

Above: Winter and Reeves view the day's rushes with director Peter Hewitt

Opposite: Keanu proved that he was ready for action in *Point Break*

assassins, they meet "Melvin" the Grim Reaper (William Sadler) before being banished to Hell, where Ted faces constant press-ups and Bill is continually kissed by his 88-year-old grandmother. Enlisting the help of the Grim Reaper, the pair visit Heaven where they gain God's support in overcoming their evil adversaries and return to San Dimas to defeat the "Evil Us's".

According to British director Peter Hewitt, neither Reeves nor Winter had any problem reprising their roles. "They do have their Bill and Ted characters locked down by now," he said. "Most of the time all I did was sit back, watch, and laugh out loud. Both are so good at playing those characters they'd mess around off camera also."

Just as Bill and Ted's debut adventure had problems making it to the big screen, so did their second outing. Test audiences didn't like Hewitt's first cut, which contained a great deal of dark and twisted humour. As a result, several sequences set in Hell were cut, including one scene in which Bill and Ted are given hammers by demon guards and bash each other endlessly. The punchline is that they enjoy it so much that they nearly decide to stay.

The ending also had to be re-shot, as viewers didn't like the original climax, in which an army of Bill and Teds from various points in the future travelled to San Dimas to save the day. Reeves himself was disappointed by the way the the film was re-cut and re-shot and refers to it as "Bill and Ted's Omitted Journey".

Although the film lacks much of the charm, vibrancy and energy of Bill and Ted's first outing, *Bogus Journey* still contained some hilarious and innovative moments. Reeves and Winter are both delightful in their familiar roles, but William Sadler steals the show as the Grim Reaper. The sight of Bill and Ted challenging "His Royal Deathness" to play board games like Cluedo, Battleships and Twister is worth the price of admission alone!

Reeves was briefly involved with the short-lived but surprisingly entertaining children's cartoon series, *Bill and Ted's Excellent Adventures*, which allowed the bodacious time-travellers to continue their exploits every Saturday morning. Both actors turned down the opportunity to star in the even shorter-lived spin-off TV series, and were replaced by Evan Richards and Christopher Kennedy. As far as Reeves was concerned, his dangerous days as a dim-witted dude were over.

Off the screen, the actor continued to hit the headlines for his motorcycling adventures. Between 1991 and 1992, reports claimed that he was stopped three times for driving with a suspended licence and had been arrested in Santa Monica for dangerous driving.

Beside his high-profile projects, Reeves starred in two student films, *Madison Avenue Clown* and *Contenders* (neither of which has been displayed widely). He also featured in the pop video for Paula Abdul's "Rush, Rush" and appeared in a video for Tom Petty after the pop star came to the actor's assistance when his motorcycle broke down in the desert.

Keanu's appearances in pop videos, coupled with his constant bouts of air guitar both on and off the screen, encouraged him to pursue his own musical career. Having spent several years teaching himself how to play the Bass guitar, Reeves decided to form the four-piece band, known as "Dogstar", with fellow actor and hockey player Robert Mailhouse. While Reeves provided the bass, Mailhouse played the drums, Bret Domrose served as the group's guitarist and Gregg Miller was responsible for vocals.

Originally described as "Nirvana mixed with the Sex Pistols", Dogstar later became "more poppy", moving away from "folk punk" towards "folk pop." Reeves has a simple but touching philosophy about life with Dogstar: "It's fun to play, we're not bad and we get free beer."

GREAT
EXPECTATIONS

Great Expectations

Reeves remains committed to playing challenging roles in ambitious projects

Having successfully proved his worth as a romantic lead and action hero, Keanu remained committed to playing challenging roles in ambitious projects. Sometimes, the risk paid off. On other occasions, it didn't.

Reeves was desperate to star in *Bram Stoker's Dracula* simply because of the film's legendary director, Francis Ford Coppola (forever remembered for his work on *The Godfather* trilogy and *Apocalypse Now*), and eventually landed a part in the film. Before shooting commenced, Reeves joined the movie's main cast at Coppola's family home in the Napa Valley, California, where they spent a week rehearsing scenes and discussing their characterisations. Keanu was immediately impressed by the revolutionary film-maker. "He's a remarkable man who lives a remarkable life," said Reeves "He's inventive and creative."

Originally titled *Dracula: The Untold Story*, Coppola's lavish gothic horror movie strives to be faithful to Bram Stoker's original 1897 novel, which the director felt had never been brought to the screen correctly. The film opens in the 15th Century, when Vlad the Impaler (Gary Oldman) returns from defeating the Turks only to discover that his beloved fiance Elisabeta (Winona Ryder) was falsely informed of his death and has committed suicide. Consumed with grief and anger, Vlad decides to denounce God and becomes Dracula, a disciple of the devil with magical powers at his disposal.

Four centuries later, Dracula learns that his Elisabeta has been reincarnated as Mina (also played by Ryder) and heads for London to win her love. Reeves co-stars as Jonathan Harker, Mina's unfortunate fiance who is imprisoned by the Count in his Transylvanian Castle and attacked by a hungry trio of blood-sucking vampirettes.

Bram Stoker's Dracula looks magnificent but received mixed critical and public acclaim. While Oldman, Ryder and Anthony Hopkins (who plays the vampire hunter Van Helsing) deliver adequate performances, Reeves is woefully miscast in an underwritten and uninteresting role.

"I was bad in that," the actor later admitted. "I didn't have the juice. My colleagues in the cast – Anthony Hopkins, Gary Oldman, Winona Ryder – were beautifully operatic. I wound up with opera envy."

Most cinemagoers were unconvinced by the actor's attempt at an English accent and would have preferred if he had simply declared that Count Dracula was a "most heinous dude." During test screenings, audiences laughed every time Reeves spoke and he had to re-dub his dialogue three times before the film was released. "I wasn't very good in Dracula to begin with so I don't think that helped," he stated.

Critics around the world mocked Keanu's performance, but the actor handled the situation well. He made no excuses and eventually began to see the funny side of his predicament. For instance, on MTV's Movie Show he joked about an occasion when he was in Los Angeles and a beggar recognised him from the film. "This guy asked me for a dollar and he goes, 'Hey, you were in Dracula. I don't care what they said, man. You were good!'"

Bruised but not beaten, Reeves returned to the big screen in *Much Ado About Nothing* a sun-soaked, sumptuous and extremely accessible adaptation of Shakespeare's play, directed by Britain's Kenneth Branagh (*Henry V*, *Mary Shelley's Frankenstein*). As the dastardly Don John, the actor tricks Prince Claudio (Robert Sean Leonard) into believing that his fiancee, Hero (Kate

Top: Jonathan Harker (Reeves) is held "prisoner" by Count Dracula (Gary Oldman) in *Bram Stoker's Dracula*

Above: Harker is seduced by a hungry trio of blood-sucking vampirettes

Opposite: Jonathan's impending marriage to Mina (Winona Ryder) is jeopardised by the evil Count Dracula

Top: Reeves joins the impressive cast of Kenneth Branagh's acclaimed adaptation of Shakespeare's *Much Ado About Nothing*

Above: The actor cuts a dashing figure of evil as the dastardly Don John

Opposite: Reeves as Julian Gitche in Gus Van Sant's *Even Cowgirls Get the Blues.* Dig those sideburns

Beckinsale) has been having an affair, while Benedict (Branagh) and Beatrice (Emma Thompson) argue their way through events in a feeble effort to disguise the fact that they really love each other.

Much Ado About Nothing was shot in Tuscany, Italy in the Summer of 1992, during which time Reeves shared a 300-year-old three-floored villa with co-stars Leonard and Beckinsale. "They put newspaper down for me in the kitchen in case I made a mess," he told a reporter. "It was great."

According to Reeves, making the film was an equally pleasant experience. "The sun was shining, we'd be sitting together waiting for our horses to drink before another go against the road and we'd be hearing stories," he revealed. "I mean, there were extraordinary personalities, you know, like Brian Blessed."

However, Reeves did have an embarrassing experience with one of the film's "extraordinary personalities", Richard Briers (a famous British comedy actor). When the teen idol asked to borrow some Italian currency from his co-star, Briers didn't recognise him and demanded to know who he was before he parted with the cash!

While the aspiring thespian's performance in *Much Ado About Nothing* received a mixed response from critics (most of whom accused him of taking things too seriously and looking uncomfortable in the role) it was nevertheless an improvement over *Bram Stoker's Dracula*. It also gave him the opportunity to learn how to ride a horse,

something he continues to do as a hobby.

Following his working holiday in Tuscany, Reeves agreed to play a small role in *Even Cowgirls Get the Blues*, Gus Van Sant's first film after *My Own Private Idaho*. Based on the 1976 cult book by Tom Robbins, it follows the adventures of former model Sissy Hankshaw (Uma Thurman), who uses her abnormally large thumbs to hitch-hike across America. During her travels, she encounters Julian Gitche (Reeves), an asthmatic artist based in New York City, and teams up with a bunch of tough cowgirls led by Bonanza Jellybean (Rain Phoenix, sister of the later River).

Even Cowgirls Get the Blues was condemned by American critics and cinemagoers, forcing Van Sant to drastically re-cut the film prior to its international release. Even in its new, supposedly improved form, it was considered to be a complete and utter disaster which failed to deliver on any dramatic or comedic level.

Reeves makes a mercifully brief appearance as Julian, and is merely required to sport a checkered jacket, large bow tie and dubious sideburns before collapsing with an unconvincing asthma attack. As in *Dangerous Liaisons*, Reeves once again manages to let Uma Thurman slip through his fingers. The actor was aware of the film's failure and reportedly said of the re-vamped European version, "My part has been gratefully cut down."

Reeves made a similar contribution to *Hideous Mutant Freekz* as a favour to his friend and former co-star, Alex Winter (Bill S. Preston Esquire himself!). Co-written and co-directed by Winter and his business partner Tom Stern, *Hideous Mutant Freekz* toplines Alex Winter as Rick Coogin, an arrogant Hollywood star who agrees to travel to Santa Flan to promote a bio-genetic fertilizer, Zygrot-24, which is actually a toxic chemical. Whilst en route to Santa Flan, Rick and his travelling partner Ernie (Michael Stoyanov) are talked into visiting a freak show, where their product transforms them into the Hideous Mutant Freekz of the title.

Together with former A-Team star Mr T (who plays The Bearded Lady) and Brooke Shields (who appears as herself), Keanu Reeves makes an uncredited cameo as Ortiz

Great Expectations

the Dog Boy. Heavily disguised and virtually unrecognisable, Reeves has little to do other than demonstrate his ability to scratch behind his ears with his leg.

Juvenile, uninvolving and unappealing, this *Mutant Freekz* show died a quick death at the box office and received a half-hearted video release across Europe in 1995, where it was retitled, *Freaked*. Judging by the fortunes of *Even Cowgirls Get The Blues* and *Hideous Mutant Freekz*, the moral is simple: if you want a successful movie, by all means let Keanu Reeves take a starring role but whatever you do don't even think about letting him make a cameo!

Keanu Reeves' next movie, Bernardo Bertolucci's $40 million Himalayan epic *Little Buddha* provided him with his most ambitious and surprising role to date. The film tells the modern day story of Dean and Lisa Conrad (Chris Isaak and Bridget Fonda), whose young son Jesse (Alex Wiesndanger) is believed to be the reincarnation of a revered Himalayan lama. In a series of flashbacks, it also depicts the fable of Prince Siddhartha (Reeves) who turned his back on a life of luxury some 2,500 years ago to go in search of enlightenment and subsequently became Buddha.

Little Buddha started life as a 50-page story by Bertolucci, which was developed into a screenplay by Rudy Wurlitzer and Mark Peploe. A Buddhist since the age of 21, Bertolucci felt that *Little Buddha*, together with his earlier films *The Last Emperor (1987)* and *The Sheltering Sky (1990)*, formed a trilogy of movies against "unchecked consumerism". In 1991, he travelled to Vienna with the film's producer Jeremy Thomas, to meet the Dali Lama, who gave his blessing to the project.

Bertolucci always believed that the hardest aspect of bringing his tale to life would be the casting of Prince Siddhartha. He had spent months auditioning Asian actors when he suddenly had the idea of talking to the part-Chinese, part-Hawaiian, part-European actor Keanu Reeves about the role.

"As soon as we met I was struck by his extreme openess," said Bertolucci. "I don't know if his inner life was complicated or not but his face, his eyes and his movements revealed the most perfect innocence.

Little Buddha starred Keanu Reeves as Prince Siddhartha, the founder of Buddhism. Director Bernardo Bertolucci felt that he would be able to portray Siddhartha's innocence perfectly

Imagine a young man of 29 who has never left home, who does not know the meaning of the words 'old age', 'sickness' or 'death'. Siddhartha was as innocent as that and Keanu convinced me he could be that person." While the director became convinced that Keanu was the actor who could bring Prince Siddhartha to life, the Hollywood star

was initially reluctant to take the role.

"To begin with, I was resistant to the story and was trying to understand it intellectually," he explained. "Bernardo taught me to be more open. I realised the film would not be so much a biography of Siddhartha but a representation of him, his life and his principles – a fable, in fact."

using a body double to depict Siddhartha's ascetic period, Reeves went on a harsh diet and lost more than two stones to play those scenes himself.

Reeves has frequently said that he was "touched but not converted" by Buddhism during the making of *Little Buddha*. Unlike a lot of his friends, he has not meditated or pursued any mystical activities since he finished working on the film.

"The most mystical thing I have is a deodorant crystal," he told *Sky* magazine. "It's a crystal, you wet it and rub it on under your arm and it acts as a deodorant. I haven't used it yet, but you rub it in your armpit and your crotch area and you are smell free!"

Both Reeves and Bertolucci hoped that *Little Buddha* would reach a mass audience and were gravely disappointed when the film was largely ignored by audiences around the world. Most of the movie's problems lie with Bertolucci's dual storyline, which melds the potentially fascinating tale of the founding of Buddhism with an uninteresting and irrelevant contemporary plot. The film also lacks drama and fails to capture Siddhartha's torment over his difficult choice between family and spirituality.

Complete with bronze tan and six wigs, Reeves certainly looks the part as the otherworldly Siddhartha and acquits himself well in such a difficult role, but his Indian accent clearly waivers on several occasions and invokes extremely unpleasant memories of *Bram Stoker's Dracula*. Nevertheless, while *Little Buddha* is littered with faults, Reeves is not one of them.

Following his work on *Little Buddha*, Reeves took a break from acting and spent most of his time performing with Dogstar. Despite his numerous achievements, he was still not in a position to demand whatever role he wanted and remained at the whim of producers and directors. Thus, when he auditioned for the lead role in a low-budget baseball comedy, *The Scout*, he was beaten by the relatively unknown Brendan Fraser. Apparently, the producers wanted an actor who was taller than 6 foot and Reeves had missed the role quite literally by an inch!

Rejected but not dejected, Reeves had to console himself with the lead role in an action film entitled *Speed*.

For Reeves, *Little Buddha* represented an "unprecedented spiritual search" and making the film proved to be a remarkable experience. With the help of his technical advisor, Dzongsar Khyentse Rinpoche, the actor learned about transcendental meditation and read the Buddhist texts. While the film's producer had originally envisaged

Great Expectations

Siddhartha decides to leave his family and home to search for enlightenment. For Keanu, *Little Buddha* represented an "unprecedented spiritual search" and the actor later revealed that he felt "touched but not converted" by Buddhism

FAST ACTION HERO

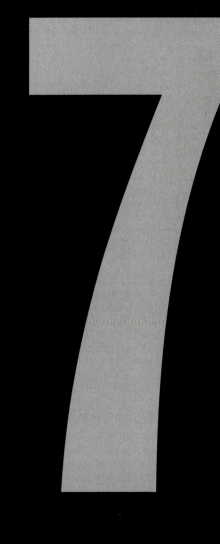

Speed transformed Keanu Reeves into an action hero and a bona fide superstar

Having worked as a cinematographer on such action films as *Die Hard*, *The Hunt For Red October* and *Lethal Weapon 3*, Jan De Bont seemed like a perfect choice to helm *Speed*, Fox's *Die Hard*-style action movie which would mark his directorial debut. De Bont was determined to dispense with many of the regular conventions of the genre and felt that it was essential to cast a "new face" in the film's leading role, as opposed to hiring an established action hero along the lines of Mel Gibson, Bruce Willis, Arnold Schwarzenegger or Sylvester Stallone.

Keanu Reeves had first come to De Bont's attention in *Point Break* and he sent the actor a copy of the script for *Speed* to see what he thought. When the pair met to discuss the project, it became clear that they shared the same vision of what the film should – and shouldn't – be.

While Reeves loved *Speed*'s "wonderfully silly premise", he told De Bont that several elements of the script "just didn't work." The actor felt that much of the dia-

Fast Action Hero

logue was quite awful and that many of main character Jack Traven's snappy one-liners were inappropriate and unbelievable. He argued that Bruce Willis's wise-cracking supercop John McClane could make jokes in *Die Hard* because the premise was treated very seriously, whereas the premise in *Speed* was so over the top that Traven had to be deadly serious in order to make the film believable. Reeves also hated the revelation that Traven's partner, Harry, was the mad bomber. De Bont agreed with Reeves's points and hired screenwriter Ross Whedon to iron out the script's imperfections and create a badder-than-bad bad guy.

"He [De Bont] wanted to make it really pure," Reeves told *Premiere* magazine. "He wanted the bad guys to be bad and good guys to be good."

De Bont was also determined to make sure that *Speed* was utterly believable. "Most action films are so elaborate with so much fantasy, you can't go along with them," he said. "*Speed* is about these normal every-day people on their regular bus ride downtown who are suddenly faced with their worst nightmare."

Although De Bont was convinced that Keanu Reeves was the perfect choice for the film's lead role, Fox executives pointed out that he had never toplined a blockbuster and were willing to trust the Dutch director provided he teamed the actor with a famous (and extremely bankable) leading lady. When De Bont decided on Sandra Bullock, whose only real claim to fame was saving the future with Sylvester Stallone in *Demolition Man*, the studio asked him to find someone else. De Bont refused, maintaining that Reeves and Bullock were "the perfect combination" and gave the film a "contemporary look and attitude". Fox continually suggested that he should recast the role, but the director stood his ground and made sure that when shooting started, Bullock was behind the steering wheel. Fortunately for De Bont, Fox had no problems accepting veteran screen actor Jeff Daniels and the legendary Dennis Hopper in the film's supporting roles.

Speed opens with L.A.P.D. cop Jack Traven (Reeves) and his faithful partner Harry (Daniels) rushing to the aid of a group of innocent hostages who are being held to ransom by a crazed bomber, Howard Payne (Hopper). When Traven manages to thwart his plans, Payne vows revenge and, shortly after, informs the fearless cop that he has placed a bomb on a bus. Once the vehicle travels at less than 50mph, the bomb will detonate, thus killing the innocent passengers. Traven manages to work his way onto the bus and, with feisty passenger Annie (Bullock) behind the wheel, tries to find a non-explosive solution to the crisis.

Keanu spent two months 'pumping iron' at Gold's Gym in L.A. to develop his arms and chest, and also took gymnastics classes three times a week to make sure he made a convincing action man. He also spent time rehearsing moves with the film's stunt co-ordinator, Gary Hymos, and discussed police procedure with the film's technical advisor, Randy Walker, who spent 21 years as an officer with the L.A.P.D. and previously worked with the actor on *Point Break*.

Two weeks before filming commenced, De Bont sent Reeves to a hairdresser's for his famous crew-cut, which the director felt would make the actor look more like a "young adult". While Reeves approved of his new image, Fox executives were furious; some suggested that Reeves should wear a wig, whilst others proposed that filming should be postponed until his locks had grown back. Once again, the director refused to budge and Keanu began work on the film on schedule and without the benefit of any hair extensions.

Speed was shot in 15 weeks, seven of which were devoted to filming the bus sequences in various locations in and around Los Angeles. The doomed bus was actually 12 identical vehicles, each designed for different uses and purposes. For instance, the most frequently used bus, dubbed "The Pope Mobile", had an enclosed Plexiglas platform fitted on its front which held cameras, operators and sound equipment and was controlled by a stunt driver seated on top of the bus. Thus, Sandra Bullock only had to pretend to be driving the vehicle, although she claimed that "It's harder than it sounds".

Whilst starring in *Point Break*, Reeves discovered that doing his own stunts allowed him to understand his character's

Top: **Jack Traven (Reeves) discovers that Howard Payne (Dennis Hopper) has taken his partner Harry (Jeff Daniels) hostage in *Speed***

Centre: **Traven risks life and limb to jump onto the speeding bus**

Above: **Director Jan de Bont discusses an upcoming scene with Keanu**

▶▶

Traven is lowered under the bus in *Speed* in a desperate attempt to defuse the bomb as the vehicle continues to travel above 50 mph

Many shared Sandra Bullock's view that Keanu had redefined the superhero

motivation and situation better and consequently give a better performance. In *Speed*, the actor performed 90 per cent of his own stunts, including the memorable sequence in which Traven jumps from a convertible Jaguar onto the speeding bus.

"In *Speed*, I really wanted to express the exertion, you know, show the audience the sheer physical effort it takes to get under a moving bus," Reeves explained to reporters. "I wanted to make these really stupid faces like, this is crazy."

Sandra Bullock was impressed by her leading man's decision to perform his own stunts and felt that it made the film "much more believable than seeing this bus hurtling down the street with a stuntman's body and Keanu's face inserted in close-up,"

An enjoyably relentless rollercoaster of a bus, train and elevator ride, *Speed* is guaranteed to get the adrenaline flowing and showcases Reeves's charismatic appeal. Within minutes, the actor blasts any remaining memory of those excellent Valley Dudes Ted and Tod away and more than lives up to the promise he showed in *Point Break*. Hopper, Bullock and Daniels are all great in their supporting roles while Jan De Bont is a revelation at the helm and manages to sustain a breath-taking momentum throughout the film. Nail-biting, exciting and thrilling, *Speed* is nothing short of an action movie masterpiece.

Despite stiff opposition from such films as *Forrest Gump*, *True Lies* and *The Lion King*, *Speed* proved to be a runaway success at the box office in 1994, grossing $121.2 million in the US, £10.1 million in the UK and more than $300 million around the world. Keanu Reeves found himself thrust into the "superstar" bracket and signed a lucrative development deal with Fox. His asking price per movie rocketed from $1 million to an extremely lucky $7 million. ("Maybe for *Speed 2* I am worth it," he said, "But maybe not.") , ranking him alongside the likes of fellow movie stars Clint Eastwood, Dustin Hoffman, Richard Gere,

Michelle Pfeiffer, Sharon Stone and Val "Batman" Kilmer.

Reeves was also widely touted as "the next action hero" and was offered a series of roles originally written with Arnold Schwarzenegger, Bruce Willis, Wesley Snipes, Steven Seagal and Jean-Claude Van Damme in mind. British action magazine *Impact* named Reeves their No.1 action hero while many shared Sandra Bullock's view that "Keanu had redefined the superhero." However, Reeves was quick to quash rumours that he would devote himself to action movies and categorically stated, "I have no real ambition to become an action hero and repeat that kind of work". On a separate occasion, he stated, "I prefer Shakespeare to the action stuff".

As the press probed into Keanu's private life for headline-worthy titbits, reports revealed that his estranged father, Samuel Nowlin Reeves, was serving a ten-year prison sentence in Hawaii for drug offences and incorrectly claimed that Keanu himself had also been imprisoned for traffic offences!

In an attempt to capitalise on the huge success of *Speed* and win some easy publicity, the Art Centre College of Design in Pasadena, California launched a course entitled "The Films Of Keanu Reeves", in which students considered his unique style of method acting. Reeves subsequently revealed that he found the idea intriguing, flattering and highly amusing.

Despite all the media attention, Reeves was determined that the success of *Speed* would not change his life and, almost as if to prove this, he arrived in the United Kingdom in October 1994 sporting a black eye from a recent hockey game. He also scoffed at reports that his crew cut had set a trend and thousands of young men across the country, including tennis player Andre Agassi and former Take That star Robbie Williams, were telling their hairdressers, "I'll have a Keanu". "That's ridiculous," he laughed. Ridiculous Keanu, but true.

Above: **Traven and Annie (Sandra Bullock) manage to escape from the bus in one piece, but their troubles are far from over**

Opposite: **Traven leads the evacuation of the bus in *Speed***

LIFE IN THE FAST LANE

8

Keanu Reeves stars as Johnny, the ultimate information courier, in the sci-fi action adventure *Johnny Mnemonic*

Following the success of *Speed*, Keanu Reeves found himself inundated with multi-million dollar film offers. Rather than sitting back on his laurels or taking the most lucrative options, he chose to keep to his original schedule and headed for the Manitoba Theatre Centre in Winnipeg, Canada, where he faced potential ridicule and earned the minimum Equity rate of pay in a low-budget stage production of *Hamlet*.

For Reeves, the appeal of playing the title role in Hamlet was obvious. "I love the

play, I love acting in Shakespeare, it's the best part in Western drama and I found a theatre that was gonna let me play it," he said. Furthermore, the project reunited Keanu with his drama school mentor Lewis Baumander, who cast him as Mercutio in a production of *Romeo and Juliet* some 12 years earlier.

The actor reportedly ignored the advice of his management to take the role and tried to keep a low profile. He wouldn't give any interviews or participate in any photo calls;

Life in the Fast Lane

"It was a very physical film for me," said Reeves of his role in *Johnny Mnemonic*

follow his activities outside of the theatre.

In January 1995, Reeves made his debut as Hamlet to a mixed response. According to the local newspaper *The Ottawa Citizen*, Reeves gave an interesting but not entirely successful performance and "simply lacks the equipment to support such a role," while at the other extreme, Britain's *The Sunday Times* theatre critic Roger Lewis wrote, "He was wonderful . . . He is one of the top three Hamlets I have seen, for a simple reason: he is Hamlet." Regardless of which review was more accurate, Reeves nevertheless managed to show the world that he remained committed to his craft.

The following month, Reeves was back on the big screen in *Johnny Mnemonic*, the film which he had shot one-and-half months after he wrapped *Speed*. Adapted by acclaimed science fiction author William Gibson (the father of "cyberpunk") from his own 22-page short story, the offbeat science fiction action-adventure movie marked the directorial debut of Robert Longo, an artist who only had a few R.E.M. and Megadeth pop videos to his credit.

Longo and Gibson started work on *Johnny Mnemonic* in 1989 and originally envisaged it as a $1.5 million black and white art house movie with Val Kilmer, Christian Slater or Johnny Depp in the title role. Reeves first heard about the project when he was shooting *Speed* and convinced Longo and Gibson to meet up with him in L.A. to discuss the film. Shortly after, Reeves was offered the role of Johnny, the high-tech information courier described in Gibson's

his first and only priority was to give a good performance. Every day, he walked to work through the Winnipeg snow and developed a good rapport with his fellow actors and theatre staff.

Despite his good intentions, however, Reeves couldn't escape from the fact that he had become a leading international star. All 22,000 seats for the three-week run of the play were sold via subscription before the box office had officially opened, and the local press started a "Keanu hotline" to

Above: With less than 24 hours to live, Johnny hires Jane (Dina Meyer) to be his bodyguard

65

Life in the Fast Lane

"Instead of looking at the technology, you get to be in it"

Above: With only hours left to live, Johnny turns to J-Bone (Ice-T) and the Loteks for help

Right: Johnny prepares to enter cyberspace

In *Johnny Mnemonic*, Reeves stars as the eponymous bio-enhanced information courier who earns his living by storing information in his own computer-enhanced mind. When Johnny exceeds his storage capacity to carry some top-secret information, he only has 24 hours to deliver the encrypted information, after which time he will suffer a complete neural failure.

Unfortunately for Johnny, several of the world's most powerful groups want the data stored in his mind and the courier soon finds himself being pursued by members of the all-powerful Yakuza as well as the "Street Preacher" (Dolph Lundgren), an unstoppable, Bible-quoting bounty hunter. As the story unfolds, Johnny finds help in the form of a software-enhanced bodyguard, Jane (Meyer), who leads him to "Heaven", the hide-out of the Loteks, a group of anarchists led by J-Bone (Ice-T).

Johnny Mnemonic was shot in 12 weeks in various locations in Montreal and Toronto, Canada, and is visually spectacular. "The film is very graphic, much like my [art] work," said Longo. "It's solid and straightforward so that you can follow the story – a story that should be told."

William Gibson was amazed by the way his vision of the future had been brought to the screen. "I was speechless," he stated. "The first time I saw the set, I was on the verge of tears for about two hours. I went away and realised that for 13 years I've gone on describing environments like this, and I never expected to see one realised to this degree of resolution."

Unfortunately, the film's stunning visuals aren't matched by its script which promises to be a high-tech version of *The Fugitive* and *D.O.A.* but manages to eradicate all trace of excitement very early on and soon becomes tedious. As the minutes pass slowly by, it becomes painfully obvious that the movie is a 22-page short story stretched beyond the

short story as "your basic sharp-faced Caucasoid with a ruff of stiff dark hair".

In a situation that was virtually identical to what had happened when *Speed* was in pre-production, the film's producer was reluctant to accept Dina Meyer as the film's leading lady. At the time, the New York-born actress had only guest-starred in a few episodes of *Beverly Hills 90210*. "My agent called them up and they wanted a name for the part," explained Meyer. "She spoke to the producer, who said, 'Dina who?'" Fortunately, the actress managed to get an audition and convinced the producer she was the right choice for the role.

Meyer enjoyed working with Reeves but found him extremely introverted. "He's a charming guy and he's very nice and soft-spoken," she said. "He's a dear person and there's so much going on inside of him, it's really hard to get it out of him."

▶▶

realms of all possible interest. Things go from bad to worse during the film's second half, when Johnny meets his potential saviour: Jones, a techno-enhanced, armour-plated war machine junkie dolphin.

Reeves delivers a fine performance as a character who is, well, deliberately characterless, and captures Johnny's mental breakdown beautifully. As in *Speed*, the actor performed most of his own stunts.

"It was a physical film for me," he said. "I had a few intense fight scenes, and I did a lot of running around on top of the Heaven sets, fighting all the bad guys . . . It was fun."

For the sequences in which Johnny enters virtual reality, Reeves studied the art of mime. "You get a different perspective," the actor explained. "Instead of looking at the technology, you get to be in it."

Despite Reeves's enthusiasm for the film, *Johnny Mnemonic* failed to consolidate his success in *Speed*. Not only was the film widely disliked (most critics referred to it as "Johnny Moronic") but it also bombed at the box office.

Although Reeves was disappointed by the film's failure, he was more upset by the way it was treated by the studio. Following its world premiere in Japan, Columbia Tri-Star decided to re-cut the film to make it into more of a action movie and re-shot its opening scene: originally, Johnny had erased his childhood memories to give himself a greater storage capacity, but thanks to the studio, he suddenly decided that he wanted his memory back (which of course contradicts the rest of the film's storyline). "It's a very different movie," says Reeves of the film in its released form.

The actor's next big screen outing following *Johnny Mnemonic* took him back in time to the year 1945 for *A Walk in the Clouds*. Based on the Italian novel *Four Steps in the Clouds*, the film had been in development since 1987 when it was

pushed into production by Fox following the successful release of *Speed*. Directed by Alfonso Arau (who helmed the highest grossing foreign film of all time, *Like Water For Chocolate*), the movie began shooting on July 27th, 1994 in the Napa Valley, California, more than a year before the film was actually released.

According to Arau, *A Walk in the Clouds* is a fairy-tale romance. "The most important thing in this film is love," he explained. "I liked the idea of the family, the traditional values, their attachment to the Earth, and the period, 1945, in which the film is set."

Having filmed *Speed* and *Johnny Mnemonic* virtually back-to-back, Reeves decided it was time for a change of pace and was keen to star in the film. "I was attracted to *A Walk in the Clouds* because I really wanted to do a romance, something that concerned itself more with the heart and sensuality," he explained. "I also shared Alfonso's interest in evoking emotions."

A Walk in the Clouds toplines Reeves as Paul Sutton, a young and idealistic American G.I. who returns from the Second World War to start a new life as a chocolate salesman. When he meets Victoria Aragon (Aitana Sanchez-Gijon), the pregnant and unmarried daughter of a proud vineyard owner, he

agrees to temporarily pose as her husband – until, that is, the pair start to fall in love.

A good old-fashioned love story, *A Walk in the Clouds* is a predictable but pleasant time-waster, which made a comfortable profit at the box office. Both Reeves and Sanchez-Gijon are charming in undemanding roles, while Anthony Quinn is a delight as the patriarchal Don Pedro.

Arau felt that the film marked Reeves's first truly adult role. Prior to starting work on the movie, the actor studied photographs of the Second World War and talked to a marine in order to understand his character's motivation and sensitivities.

For Keanu, the biggest challenge wasn't making Paul Sutton believable, but filming a love scene with his co-star Debra Messing. The night before the scene was shot, Reeves was playing hockey when a teammate accidentally hit him in the face with a hockey stick. As a result, the star required six stitches inside and outside his mouth. "It was so sad," said Messing. "We had to do a lot of kissing . . . He kept saying 'Please don't hurt me!'"

As filming continued, rumours began to circulate in the tabloid press and several of the teen magazines that the producers had ordered Reeves to watch Kevin Costner movies in order to polish up his kissing technique. Several magazines also ran reports claiming that the actor had taken to wearing a skirt and combat boots in between takes.

With or without skirt, Keanu remained one of the world's popular actors in 1995. He was named the 18th most important actor in Hollywood in *Premiere* magazine's prestigious poll, which placed him above the likes of Jack Nicholson, Sharon Stone and Winona Ryder as well as his action-man rivals Bruce Willis and Steven Seagal.

Meanwhile, *Empire* magazine declared that he was the 17th sexiest movie star (and eighth sexiest male star) of all-time, beating such major heart-throbs as Mel Gibson, Tom Cruise, Steve McQueen, Cary Grant, Brad Pitt, Clark Gable and Hugh Grant. The magazine described Reeves as "Adorable" and claimed that he was better looking than British comedian Vic Reeves. High praise indeed!

Life in the Fast Lane

Top: Director Alfonso Arau instructs Reeves and Aitana Sanchez-Gijon during the filming of *A Walk in the Clouds*

Above left: Reeves attends a screening of the film with co-star Sanchez-Gijon

Above: Reeves as Paul Sutton, a young and idealistic American G.I.

Opposite: Victoria Aragon (Sanchez-Gijon) finally succumbs to Sutton's charm

KEEPING ONE STEP AHEAD

9

Reeves has avoided typecasting through a combination of careful choices and lucky breaks

During the course of his career, Keanu Reeves has risked being typecast as a thug, an alienated teenager, a dim-witted Valley dude, a romantic lead or an action hero. His burning desire to portray a wide range of characters and switch genres, coupled with some extremely fortuitous breaks and the public's constant willingness to overlook his mistakes, enable him to keep one step ahead of the Hollywood system.

Reeves spent the summer of 1995 attempting to redefine his image yet again in *Feeling Minnesota*, a low-budget noir comedy in which he plays a hopeless drifter who falls in love with his brother's wife

(played by Cameron Diaz of *The Mask* fame). His co-stars for this decidedly non-mainstream project include Vincent D'Onofrio, Dan Aykroyd and Courtney Love.

Once the film finished shooting, Reeves joined Dogstar for an international tour. The band played in 24 cities across America, spent eight days in Japan and supported Bon Jovi in Australia and New Zealand. Several major record companies attempted to offer Dogstar recording deals, some suggesting that Reeves should become its front-man, but the actor-turned-musician wasn't interested. For him, Dogstar is fun, a way of escaping the limelight and he has

▶▶

repeatedly stated that "the band is not about me."

However, whether he liked it or not, Keanu was the major selling point of the group. As the band travelled around the world, his fans flocked to see their idol in concert and also made Dogstar the first unsigned band to fill New York's Irving Plaza. Reviews of the group's performance were unexceptional at best and a reviewer for the *House of Blues* magazine summed up the general verdict when he wrote, "The group's not bad but average".

Reeves co-hosted an American TV documentary, *Children Remember The Holocaust*, before making his long-awaited return to the world of the action movie for *Dead Drop*. Directed by Andrew Davis, who helmed Steven Seagal in the surprisingly successful *Under Siege* before joining Harrison Ford for the acclaimed blockbuster *The Fugitive*, *Dead Drop* focuses on a high-tech weaponry expert who goes on the run when he discovers the government's plans for his latest invention.

Even before the first draft of its script was finished, *Dead Drop* was being touted as Keanu's biggest hit after *Speed*. However, Keanu was uninterested in such speculation. "I'm not the kind of person who gets riled over box office figures," he said. "What really interests me is just day-to-day living and being a part of the world. I'm intent on being as normal as possible in this unconventional field."

While Reeves might not get excited about box office figures, studio executives certainly do and the staff at Fox are keen for him to make a sequel to *Speed*. The actor has stated he is willing to make the film provided it has "the right script". "We'd have to push it, reinvent it," he said. "It couldn't be the same thing again."

Both Reeves and his co-star, Sandra Bullock, have joked about the premise for the sequel. Bullock suggested that Jack Traven and his pregnant wife, Annie, are visiting Paris when she announces that she's about to give birth. Using a "borrowed" ambulance, Traven must race through the streets of Paris in search of a hospital!

Reeves, on the other hand, suggested that *Speed 2* could be "an Adam and Eve thing, where we have to re-populate the world!"

A third Bill and Ted film remains a distinct possibility. While Reeves has often stated that he was disappointed by the changes made to *Bill and Ted's Bogus Journey*, he also accepts that there have been "some good sequels", such as *The Godfather Part II*, *The Evil Dead II* and the Indiana Jones films, and that he might one day reprise the role of Ted "Theodore" Logan once more. "Maybe we should wait 'til we're about 43," he quipped, "then we could do Bill and Ted's Mid-life Crisis."

When asked to consider his own career, Reeves is pleased to report that he more or less remains outside of mainstream film-making and has "settled on not settling." He feels that playing innocents is the only constant of his career and that he has almost become the male equivalent of the female ingenue. "My career through-line is innocence, in a variety of different genres."

Although Reeves has never won the widespread critical acclaim that he so desperately craves, he continues to gain fans and admirers around the world with each and every film, television and stage role. Sandra Elizabeth Kibbey of the British "Keanu Fan Network" summed up the actor's appeal by saying, "It all comes down to qualities which are difficult to define – charisma, sex appeal and star quality."

In his free time, the actor still tries to lead a "quiet, dull life away from the bright lights and parties," and has always said that he never wants to be "super-famous". "I'm frightened by the image of a 'star'," he explained. "I love my work but I'm uncomfortable with fame . . . The prospect of it getting worse fills me with dread."

Thanks to *Speed*, the actor is recognised a lot more by the public ("Usually people come up to me and say, 'Weren't you the guy from *Speed*?' and then we talk about the film"), but still tries to keep a low profile and says that he is more likely to be followed around town by the press than by fans.

As if to illustrate his point, Reeves was caught on camera in December 1995, enduring a customs search at L.A.'s International Airport. Apparently, the actor had turned

Keeping One Step Ahead

Above: Although he has no desire to quit acting, Keanu continues to play bass guitar with Dogstar and is seen here performing at Trade Winds in New Jersey

down V.I.P. treatment and would also have faced a bag search, if he had possessed any luggage!

Many people have suggested that Reeves's discomfort with stardom and his old-fashioned desire to keep his private life private only contributes to this appeal. As his *Speed* co-star Sandra Bullock once pointed out, "Everything about him is laced with mystery – that's his charm."

Looking ahead, Reeves says that his only firm plans are to keep acting and to continue to play a diverse range of roles. "I'd like to do a lot of different things," he explained. "That's the challenge, the test, the scary part and also the interesting aspect of acting."

While he might one day turn his attention to writing poetry and plays, Reeves has no intention of following in the footsteps of actor-turned-President Ronald Reagan or spear-heading any political or moral campaigns. "I'm making movies in Hollywood, you know," Reeves told *Interview* magazine. "The things that I'm doin' are pretty sheltered. For me, acting is very self-involved, especially between projects. Once you get a part, you're liberated. You can find out what your character thinks."

Keanu Reeves has come a long way since starring in Coca-Cola and Kelloggs' Cornflake adverts and has promised his fans that he will continue to work until he pays off his motorcycle insurance! While he cannot quite explain or understand how he has managed to establish and maintain such a successful career, he remains modest about his achievements and is aware of just how lucky he's been.

"You know what is a nice thought?" the actor once pondered. "Retirement. That's what we've got to look forward to. A hundred movies in the can and time to relax on a warm beach."

I wouldn't pack your suntan lotion and beach towel just yet, Keanu.

FILMOGRAPHY

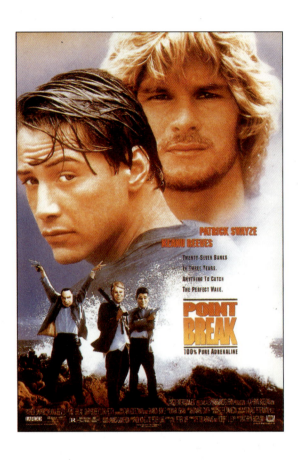

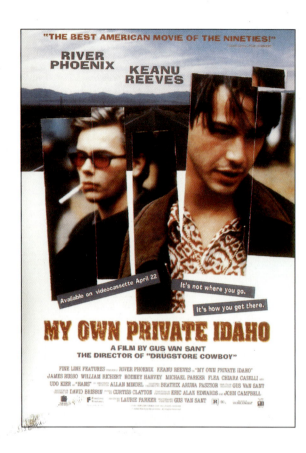

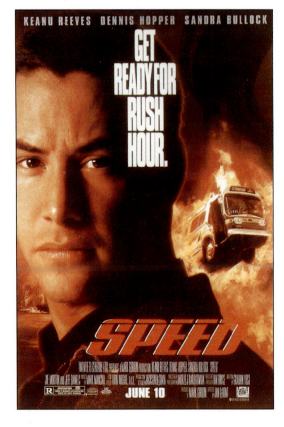

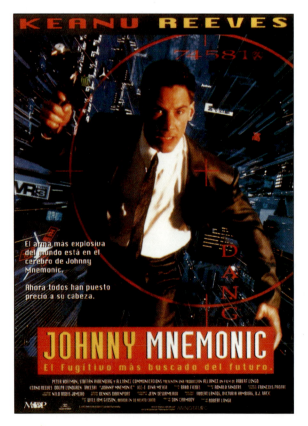

1982	*The Prodigal*
1985	*Flying* (also known as *Dream to Believe*)
1986	*Youngblood*
	Act of Vengeance (TV movie)
	The Brotherhood of Justice (TV movie)
	Under the Influence (TV movie)
	Young Again (TV movie)
	Babes in Toyland (TV movie)
	River's Edge
1988	*Permanent Record*
	The Night Before
	Dangerous Liaisons
	The Prince of Pennsylvania
1989	*Bill & Ted's Excellent Adventure*
	Parenthood
1990	*I Love You to Death*
	Tune in Tomorrow (also known as *Aunt Julia and the Scriptwriter*)
1991	*Point Break*
	My Own Private Idaho
	Bill & Ted's Bogus Journey
1992	*Bram Stoker's Dracula*
1993	*Much Ado About Nothing*
	Even Cowgirls Get the Blues
	Hideous Mutant Freekz (also known as *Freeks*)
	Little Buddha
1994	*Speed*
1995	*Johnny Mnemonic*
	A Walk in the Clouds
1996	*Feeling Minnesota*
	Chain Reaction

Television Appearances

1980	*Hangin' In'*
1984	*Night Heat*
	Letting Go

▶▶

Keanu Reeves enjoys a joke with River Phoenix and director Gus Van Sant (in the hat) during a break in the filming of *My Own Private Idaho*

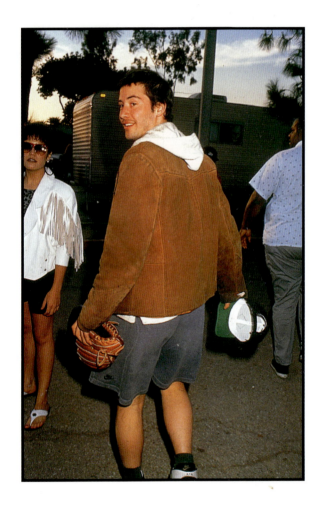